no label

The Music Box

The Story of Cristofori

Dedicated to those who long for self-expression

and wish to "say it" with music.

written by

Suzanne Guy 𝄞 Donna Lacy

illustrated by

Donna Lacy

Brunswick

Library of Congress Cataloging-in-Publication Data

Guy, Suzanne, 1941–
    The music box : the story of Cristofori / by Suzanne Guy and Donna Lacy. --
1st ed.
            p.   c.m.
    Summary: The story of Bartolomeo Cristofori, the Italian harpsichord maker who invented the piano while working in the city of Florence about three hundred years ago.
        ISBN 1-55618-172-8 (alk. paper). -- ISBN 1-55618-173-6 (pbk. : alk. paper)
        1. Cristofori, Bartolomeo, 1655–1732--Juvenile literature.   2. Harpsichord makers--Italy--Biography--Juvenile literature.   3. Piano makers--Italy--Bio-graphy--Juvenile literature.   4. Piano--History--18th century--Juvenile literature.
[1. Cristofori, Bartolomeo, 1655–1732.   2. Harpsichord makers.   3. Piano makers.   4. Piano--History.]   I. Lacy, Donna, 1952–   .   II. Title.
ML3930.C923G89   1998
786 '. 19 ' 092--dc21
    [b]
                                                                98–23309
                                                                     CIP
                                                                  AC MN

First Edition
Published in the United States of America
by

Brunswick Publishing Corporation
1386 Lawrenceville Plank Road
Lawrenceville, Virginia 23868
1-800-336-7154

There was a rainbow in the sky that day in May so long ago. The soft colors formed an arc over the small village in Italy where a little boy was born.

His parents looked at their tiny baby in the crib and decided to give him a big long name:

Bartolomeo di Francesco Cristofori
[BAR-TOE-LOW-<u>MAY</u>-O DEE FRAN-<u>CHESS</u>-KOE KRIS-<u>TOFF</u>-OR-EE]

They called him Bartolomeo for short.

In no time at all, Bartolomeo was out of the crib and into everything. His favorite place to play was the kitchen, right beside the big old fireplace where his mother kept her cooking pans.

Rattle, prattle,
bumpity bang,

Boom, bong,
clunkety clang.

What a symphony of sounds he made!

And all of it was music to Bartolomeo's ears. He loved to create — noise!

When he was a little older, Bartolomeo's noise became more inventive. He put the tiniest trinkets together to make the tiniest tinkling sounds. Then he banged and hammered big boards and wooden blocks to make loud clanging crashes!

"Music," he thought, "should make all sorts of sounds."

Bartolomeo's mother had to shout to be heard,
"I think it's time for our son to
have music lessons."

"Yes, yes," agreed his father. "Right away."

And they sent him to a very fine teacher
where he learned to play several instruments.

The years passed, and Bartolomeo grew taller. His love for music grew larger as well.

Before long he took a job making harpsichords, the most popular instrument in all the land. He was very good at his craft, so good that he was invited to work in the palace of Prince Ferdinando in the famous city of Florence.

Bartolomeo thought he was indeed lucky to work in such a beautiful palace and to make such a prized musical instrument as the harpsichord.

Even so, he was not completely satisfied.

Something wasn't right.
Something was missing.

"All these notes sound the same," he complained.

Where are the whispers?
Where are the splashes?
I can't hear the booms,
and I can't make the crashes.

And so, Bartolomeo continued his search for all sorts of sounds, sounds to match feelings, sounds that would sing.

His new friends in Florence heard the rings and zings coming from the palace workshop. "What are you making, Bartolomeo?" they asked, as they climbed on top of each other, making a human ladder to peek inside.

Bartolomeo grinned, "A magic box that will whisper, tingle, thunder, and jingle." His friends did not understand. Bartolomeo seemed to be talking in riddles.

Prince Ferdinando was also curious about Bartolomeo's hammering and pounding and the strange noises coming from the workshop.

"What are you making, Bartolomeo?" he asked. Always patient with the prince, Bartolomeo answered, "It will be a music box that can make a sound for every shade of color in the rainbow."

"H-mmm," said Prince Ferdinando.

Soon everyone was asking,
"What are you making, Bartolomeo?"

The noisy palace workshop was becoming a big
mystery in the city of Florence.

One night, when everyone else was asleep, Bartolomeo was wide awake working late. Just as he leaned over to tighten some strings, his tool bag of little hammers tumbled into the box all around him.

As the hammers fell helter-skelter against the wire strings, they created the most wonderful sounds Bartolomeo had ever heard.

"Bella Musica!"

"Little hammers, why of course, that's it."

Hammers to bounce up and hit the strings,

stoppers and dampers, some gadgety things

covered with leather, felt may work too.

I can see it and hear it, I know what to do.

Bartolomeo worked on through the night.

Finally he rubbed his eyes and looked around the room at all the pieces he had put together.

A single candle burned brightly, flickering light over 54 blocks of newly finished wood. These were the keys to his new music box. Together with the bouncing hammers and strings, they would unlock all the glorious sounds he loved so much.

As Bartolomeo squeezed the last key in place, the sun began to light the room. It was a grand new day.

He sat down at his invention and pressed a single key, softly at first, then a little harder, and a little harder still. The difference was amazing.

He leaned forward and played ten keys at the same time with all eight fingers and two thumbs.

It wasn't long before wondrous music streamed from his music box through the palace workshop window.

People passing by stopped to listen. Never before had they heard such beautiful music. Some sounds were as loud and powerful as thunder, and others were as soft and gentle as rain. And all of them came from the same instrument!

As the crowd grew, a few people swayed and hummed while others began to dance right there on the street. Soon Bartolomeo's friends arrived and, of course, they called to him, "What are you playing, Bartolomeo? Bartolomeo, what have you made?"

With a flourish, he threw open the doors to share his
new music box. "Listen, my friends, and listen again.
It has a big long name:

gravicembalo col piano e forte.

[GRAH-VEE-<u>CHEM</u>-BAH-LOW   CALL   PEA-<u>AN</u>-NO   AY   <u>FOR</u>-TAY]

But I think I'll call it a

PIANO

for short!"

More about the Story

Yes, this is a true story ... mostly. This type of writing is called historical fiction. We started with what we could learn from old records. That's the history part. Then we filled in and figured out what might have happened.

Bartolomeo was born on May 4, 1655, in Padua, a university town in Italy.

This is the only known portrait of Bartolomeo Cristofori.

Can you find Cristofori in the crowd scene?

Prince Ferdinando De' Medici
Prince Ferdinando De' Medici loved music and was a good harpsichordist himself. He employed an orchestra of full-time musicians in his court. Records show that Bartolomeo was the caretaker and maker of the palace instruments.

Wealthy men of the 17th century wore wigs, makeup, bows, and lace.

The Pitti Palace in Florence

Notes on the Piano

If you took apart a Cristofori piano, this is what one key action would look like. Compare this model from 1720 to the illustration close-up view.

The hammer mechanism invented and improved by Cristofori.

So what do HAMMERS have to do with playing the piano?

The hammers in the piano are sensitive to pressure on the keys. This makes it possible to create a wider range of expressive sound.

(1) **Press any key.**

(2) **The hammer jumps up and bounces against a wire (called a string).**

(3) **The hammer falls back in place.**

(4) **Do it all over again**

These four steps happen in less time than it takes to blink an eye.

Cristofori's piano had only 54 keys. Today's pianos usually have 88 keys.

What does *GRAVICEMBALO COL PIANO E FORTE* mean? The literal translation is "harpsichord with soft and loud."

For fun, we added cats to help express Bartolomeo's different moods in the illustrations.

Especially for $\mathcal{P}$iano $\mathcal{S}$tudents and their $\mathcal{T}$eachers

Waiting for some action ...

Notice the piano, how it sits and waits—freshly tuned and sound asleep. To many, it's a piece of furniture. To others, it's a mechanical marvel of 12,000 parts. In the hands of people who know how to make music, the piano is nothing less than a miracle.

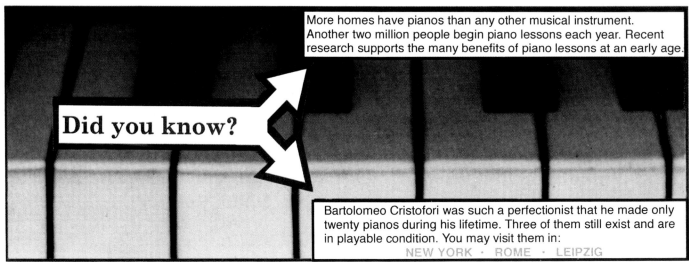

Did you know?

More homes have pianos than any other musical instrument. Another two million people begin piano lessons each year. Recent research supports the many benefits of piano lessons at an early age.

Bartolomeo Cristofori was such a perfectionist that he made only twenty pianos during his lifetime. Three of them still exist and are in playable condition. You may visit them in:

NEW YORK · ROME · LEIPZIG

Who would dream that wire strings struck by felt hammers could express all kinds of feelings?

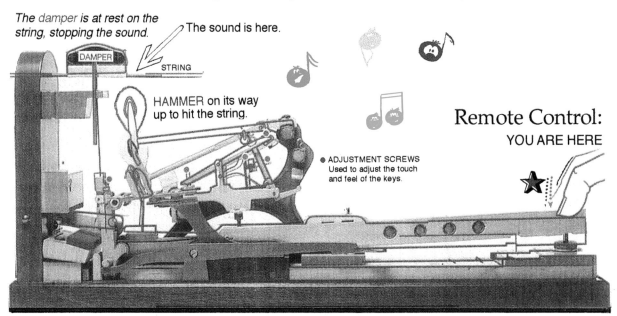

The damper is at rest on the string, stopping the sound.

The sound is here.

DAMPER

STRING

HAMMER on its way up to hit the string.

● ADJUSTMENT SCREWS
Used to adjust the touch and feel of the keys.

Remote Control:
YOU ARE HERE

The Inside View of a Steinway Piano Action

The piano is a wonderful example of remote control. What happens at the other end of the key you see is what matters. The more weight from the fingertip, the more sound when the hammer taps the string. This is the beginning of playing the piano with expression.

The amount of force used here determines the quality of sound at the moment of hammer strike.

Sources, Credits, and Bibliography

The authors wish to acknowledge the following sources of information and research. Without their contribution, this project would be incomplete and less accurate.

Museums:

Musée des instruments de musique – Brussels, Belgium.
   Photograph of hammer mechanism in Cristofori's piano – 1720.

Metropolitan Museum of Art. New York.
   Photograph of Cristofori's 1720 piano, the oldest playable piano in the world.

Smithsonian. Division of Historic Instruments. Washington, D.C.

Models:

Steinway & Sons. New York. Model of a single key action.

Books:

Acton, Harold. *The Last Medici*. New York: Thames and Hudson, 1980.

Crombie, David. *Piano.* San Francisco: Miller-Freeman Books, 1995.

Dolge, Alfred. *Pianos and Their Makers*. New York: Dover, 1972.

Gaines, James R. *The Lives of the Piano.* New York: Holt, Rinehart and Winston, 1981.

Gorsline, Douglas. *What People Wore.* New York: Bonanza Books, 1952

Janson, H. *History of Art*. New York: Prentice-Hall, Inc. and Harry N. Abrams, Inc., 1973.

Kottick, Edward L. *The Harpsichord Owner's Guide.* University of North Carolina Press, 1987.

Libin, Laurence. *Keyboard Instruments.* Metropolitan Museum of Art, pp. 34-35.

Oringer, Judith. *Passion for the Piano.* Los Angeles: Jeremy P. Tarchers, Inc., 1983.

Peacock, John. *The Chronicle of Western Fashion.* New York: Harry N. Abrams, Inc., 1991.

Unger-Hamilton, Clive. *Keyboard Instruments.* Oxford: Phaidon Press, Ltd., 1981.

Articles:

Tommasini, Anthony. Article/Diagram in *The New York Times*. "Tuning Pianos at the Juilliard School of Music." December 30, 1997.

Rohner, Ann E., Editor. *Clavier's Piano Explorer.* "The Classical Period." Northfield, Illinois. May/June 1997.

The Authors

Suzanne W. Guy

Suzanne Guy is a graduate of Agnes Scott College with a degree in Piano Performance. She has been teaching piano students for many years, and loving (almost) every minute. She has shared her joy in music and her creative approach to teaching in many ways: through piano pedagogy classes as a faculty member at Peabody Conservatory and George Mason University; through lectures and master classes across the United States and overseas; and through a regular column in *Clavier* magazine. After raising three sons in suburban Northern Virginia, Guy and her engineer husband have relocated to downtown Norfolk (moving the three cherished grand pianos), and become city dwellers.

Donna M. Lacy

Donna Lacy received her Bachelor of Arts degree in Art Education from Marshall University. She has also studied Child Development and Children's Literature in her graduate work. Certainly as formative as her classroom education has been the diversity of her life experiences. Lacy taught school in Sydney, Australia. After two years DOWN UNDER, she returned to the United States by backpacking through Asia and Europe. Along the way she had adventures, made memories, and collected interesting story ideas. Since then, Lacy has had various mini careers, all of which tied in with her primary interests of art, education, and travel. She currently resides in Virginia Beach with her husband, two children, and assorted pets.